Y0-AGK-534

HEATHER BRAGINTON-SMITH

Whispers of the World

I have no love of things —
My joy comes or came at least
in the creating of joy,
the bringing of happiness.
I was told many times I
was impossible to understand
because I loved everything
and was content without anything.
I traveled through
life like a vagabond.
Enjoying the things the
world had seemingly forgotten.
Listening to the whispers
of the world when all about
me had their stereos playing on 10.

Heather Braginton-Smith
June 13, 1959 — March 20, 1997

A PERSONAL NOTE

Browsing through the art section of a large book store or the pages of art book catalogues one sooner or later becomes aware of how many large, expensive books are devoted to the work of some single artist who really deserves little or no attention, but who happens to get it because, either calculatedly or mindlessly, a negligible talent has been pushed through a small hole, so to speak, like a pastry tube producing whatever bravura squiggles, tasteless in every sense of the word, will give a flashy desirability to a cake about which the less said the better. And of course it helps if lots of them are being iced at the same time in a place noted for just such desserts.

And then it may occur to one to wonder about other artists, much better ones who for various reasons, a lot of them fortuitous and irrelevant, but some because of their own aims, desires, and temperaments, do not have books about them, who remain far too little known for their work.

Heather Braginton-Smith has been one of these. She was fantastically talented and seemed to have an extraordinary facility that accompanied it (however difficult the work was actually to do is something we will never know) so she could turn it to almost any use from the most casual sketch on a napkin to the commercial: theatre, advertising, all sorts of miscellaneous ideas and projects to the very fine indeed; her generosity with her time and spirit led her to do a great deal of all kinds, so that her reputation as an artist has been somewhat confused and ill-defined.

Her work was not at all fashionable, seemingly more nineteenth than twentieth century in manner and feeling (though only on the surface) and ranged from story-telling pictures and fantasy, children and animals, seascapes, and trompe l'oeil in the tradition of Harnett and Peto, this her best work to my mind.

She never really set out to have a career and constantly work at it, she showed in no one gallery, and much of her work such as murals in houses and parts of stage sets is not readily available.

Heather is someone it is particularly hard to remember she is no longer with us, and this book devoted to her work, in spite of the tragedy of her early death that has occasioned it, makes her one of the lucky ones in this respect, will make it even more so.

Edward Gorey, July 1997

HEATHER BRAGINTON-SMITH

onvention has it that an artist develops and perfects one style of painting in a life time, maybe two, but certainly no more. Convention likes consistency.

Heather Braginton-Smith was, in every sense of the word, unconventional. She was intelligent and generous with a warm and quirky personality, a prolific and talented painter of many styles, a self-taught artist whose commitment to her work is evident in her life's work.

Born on Cape Cod on June 13, 1959, she was one of six children of Dorothy and Jack Braginton-Smith. At age 12, when other children were busy collecting a weekly allowance, young Heather began her first professional painting venture rendering commissioned portraits of animals and children. Later, at Dennis-Yarmouth Regional High School, the artist credited her art teacher, Mrs. Pauline Hopkins, as the one person who most encouraged and nurtured her interest in the arts.

In an interview conducted with this writer and published in *Cape Cod Antiques & Arts* in 1995, Braginton-Smith commented that she had been painting as long as she could remember. And, indeed, she tenaciously pursued painting over each successive year, continuing her self-education while raising four children — Alexandra, Phillippa, Johannah and Joshua — who now range in age from six to 14.

The artist was very clear about the enormous satisfaction she found in her dual role of mother and artist. Though she didn't gloss over the difficulties and challenges in her personal life which at that time were large, she was steadfast in her commitment to her family and her art. During the interview she was, as those who knew her well might say, "quintessentially Heather" — meaning she was at once sincere, quirky, warm, introspective, motherly, troubled, optimistic; she shared her thoughts, her humor, her art, her stories, her children with the same enthusiastic, almost innocent, passion.

The artist, buttering waffles for young Phillippa who was home from school with an earache, explained one of the ways in which she had managed to cope with the challenges of her dual role as mother and artist: "I paint in the kitchen, the center of activity. There's actually an advantage. I set up the painting on the edge of the activity, and because I'm doing so many other things, I'm not always concentrating on the painting. The advantage is that I often catch the painting out of the corner of my eye as I move around the kitchen, so I'm constantly seeing it with a fresh eye."

Working in this way for years, the artist tackled numerous projects. There were commercial illustrations for Puritan of Cape Cod; scenic designs for set designers Helen Pond and Herbert Senn; and set design and construction for other local theater groups.

Pond and Senn, Tony Award winning scenic designers, created sets at The Cape Playhouse in Dennis for years; they often commissioned Braginton-Smith. Senn recalls her skill with portraiture. A production of *Me and My Girl* came to mind. In that play, the set required four portraits of ancestors but, he reports, they had to be portraits of the four actors. The artist worked from photographs, aging her subjects appropriately and rendering the paintings in a style appropriate to the era. Then there were the two life size statues that the artist made for *La Cage Aux Folles*. There was the portrait of Doris Day for *Definitely Doris*. But Pond reckons her poster of Falstaff for *Lettice & Lovage* was one of the best she ever did.

Two years ago when Pond and Senn were working on a redesign of the set of *Nutcracker* for the Boston Ballet, they commissioned Braginton-Smith to paint the cut-out people for the boxes on either side of the proscenium. Unable to resist subtleties, the artist painted in a portrait of E. Virginia Williams, founder of the Boston Ballet, among other Ballet celebrities. "Heather had the ability to work big and to work fast," says Senn. "Many artists can't. She could also work in many styles."

Braginton-Smith's ease in working within different genres served her well in scenic design, but was a skill that made things more difficult for her in the world of fine art where traditionalists rate a signature style more highly than diversity. Not that this bothered the artist in the slightest. She was, in her art as in her life, a free spirit.

Heather Braginton-Smith was also known for her numerous donations to local causes. She donated paintings to WBGH Channel 2's "Two Collection;" the Cape Museum of Fine Arts' "Wet Art Auction;" and the Arts Foundation of Cape Cod's "Pops By The Sea." She donated her time and talent to reproducing three historic paintings stolen from the Bangs Hallet House in Yarmouth Port. Here her skills with portraiture shine.

Braginton-Smith was a teacher. In 1992 she joined the faculty of the Cape Museum of Fine Arts teaching the art of trompe l'oeil. She lectured on art at the Creative Arts Center in Chatham.

In 1989, she had her first one-person show at Craig Studios in Dennis. In 1993, the Patricia Weiner Gallery in Cincinnati, Ohio, mounted a small one-person show of her work. In that same year, the Charlotte Inn in Edgartown on Martha's Vineyard began showing and selling her work. Concurrent with the publication of this catalog, the Cape Museum of Fine Arts is mounting a retrospective of her work.

How I have loved the beauty

of the world – the spinning

sparks of life by minutes.

the silent rumble of the

wind of winter that makes

us happy to be warm blooded,

cozy – alive.

Heather Braginton-Smith

Braginton-Smith painted every day. The way she described it is that she worked hard "to make the paint just squishy enough or just liquid enough for it to sit just right." She articulated what many artists describe in one way or another: "It sounds corny, but it's almost like having a romance with the paint."

But the hardest thing to master, she said, "is the brush stroke... how to make those little hairs on a stick do exactly what I want them to do. It will take a lifetime."

Heather Braginton-Smith pursued her goal of excellence her entire life time. There were no short cuts. Hers was a trial and error journey of daily practice combined with self study. This volume is evidence of her success.

Illusion and fantasy inform many paintings by Heather Braginton-Smith. She is best known, perhaps, for her trompe l'oeil where illusion reigns. The art historic continuum from which Braginton-Smith draws inspiration is weighty and impressive, stretching back to the height of its popularity in the 17th century when visual illusion existed without title—trompe l'oeil as a label only surfaced a couple hundred years later. And whether it was a general suspicion of technical virtuosity prompted by the rise of Impressionism or, perhaps, the advent of photography, intense realism fell out of favor for decades, only to resurface sometime in the mid-20th century. Not that Braginton-Smith paid any heed to what was in or out of favor. She was simply drawn to the challenges of the genre, and mastered difficult techniques through steadfast commit-ment to her work. She achieved technical mastery, but technical mastery alone does not guarantee that a painting be successful. Braginton-Smith's great talent was combining her technical expertise with her creative flair, applying marks with her own imaginative purpose; her trompe l'oeils are ambitious and successful.

Braginton-Smith's visual make-believes lull viewers into casual consent; there is an element of unquestioning acceptance that what they see is, in fact, what is.

Violin With Bougereau, 1991, is a wonderful example. The beautifully detailed highly polished musical instrument hangs on a heavily grained wooden panel on which are pinned family "snapshots." The small, torn sheet of music in the bottom left of the picture plane begs the viewer to smooth its wrinkled edges. Like many of her paintings, the picture combines the many genres with which this artist exhibited expertise. The small "snapshots" are tiny landscapes and miniature portraits "pinned" to the exquisitely rendered trompe l'oeil.

In another, *Brewster Kitchen,* 1985, the artist takes advantage of her own environment as subject. It is quite possible this corner of the kitchen was captured spontaneously

When the sky burns with pink orange and turns the clouds to ripened plums – When the sun blazed orange and burns the sky with its light as twilight nears and the stars begin to twinkle at the last rays of a hot summer sky. . .

Heather Braginton-Smith

with very little formal arranging. It is one of her earlier works. *Brewster Kitchen* is compositionally superb. It also shows evidence of the artist's early struggles with perspective, struggles which she overcame in subsequent works.

In 1995, the artist pushed the bounds of traditional trompe l'oeil subjects, personalizing content in her wonderfully original way. A series of paintings which she called "inner portraits" are either perceptions of client or subject matter as interpreted by the artist, or collaborations between client and artist. In the latter, the two—artist and client— create a personal portrait of the person by composing and rendering objects of significance to the subject of the painting.

"To Walter With Love," an inner portrait of newscaster Walter Cronkite, is one such example. The painting includes, in Cronkite's words, "some of our favorite artifacts. It was marvelous, done in the Dutch style of the old masters."

Braginton-Smith described her inner portraits: "Rather than painting a portrait of what a person looks like, I paint the things they love and the people they love." Which is to say, Braginton-Smith painted the things that speak to whom the person really is. She painted the person's heart and soul revealed through treasured objects.

Heart and soul resonate through Braginton-Smith's paintings. No where is this more apparent than in her fantasy paintings, each of which originated in the artist's own fertile imagination.

Gift of the Great Pearl, 1988, is an excellent example. A dark and brooding work, *Pearl* illustrates the artist's story of an old man and the sea; the old man had given up all joy, having lost his wife and child to illness. He ventures into treacherous seas, battles the weather, experiences visions and, finally rescued, reveals his gift of the Great Pearl given to him by the merchildren in recognition of his long, hard years fishing. A fine painting, it demonstrates the artist's imaginative musings and reveals her painterly skills. *Pearl* was preceded by a little known painting called *Mercy,* 1987.

Not limited to fantasy and illusion, Braginton-Smith was an accomplished landscape painter, and also proficient with marine subjects and still lives; she was a skilled illustrator and superb portrait painter.

She handled paint skillfully. On the one hand, depending on subject and style, she painted works with great luminosity. Consider *Mermaids Keep* with its beautifully rendered, softly luminescent sunset. On the other hand, she moved just as freely toward dimly lit environments. *Still Life With Gourd and Grapes* comes to mind. The surface is

You hold the world

in the palm of your hand –

hold it gently. . .

Heather Braginton-Smith

dark and deep providing a rich ground for her carefully arranged, exquisitely rendered grapes and squash. The three little white blossoms almost glow in the lower right corner of the picture plane.

Braginton-Smith's mastery of these many techniques was hard earned. Much was trial and error. A painting or a technique would intrigue her and she would attempt to reproduce what she had seen. She strived for authenticity. Her ancestor portraits, for example, were often painted on old canvases already patinaed with age. Yet, just as she would master one technique, another would catch her eye.

Galleries had a hard time categorizing her work. Though admiring of her skill, they remained uncertain, fearful of embracing the unrestrained energy of a free spirit. Many encouraged her to pick a style and stay with it, something the artist steadfastly refused to do. Painting was fun for this artist and limiting herself to one style would most certainly have taken much of the fun from the process.

Her joy in process is evident in her sense of humor, the little things she often painted into a work of art "just for fun." A shadow painted within the picture plane finds its way to the frame; a fly sits annoyingly to the edge of another ("Heather as the fly on the wall," says a close friend); in her theatrical commissions, portraits resembling friends and family emerge (two small statues rendered for Cape Playhouse scenic designer Richard Chambers' production of *Nunsense* come to mind: one resembles the artist's father, Jack Braginton-Smith; the other, her mentor, Herbert Senn).

Jill Slaymaker, friend and confidant of the artist, laments that, in her estimation, Braginton-Smith didn't always value her work highly enough, handling it too casually. "She was ambivalent. On the one hand, she treated her work casually as if it were worth little; on the other hand, she felt her talent was a gift from God and that it was the greatest gift ever."

Heather Braginton-Smith shared her gifts freely, whether painting, teaching, illustrating products or just talking about her work. She was very much a part of the community in which she lived, and remains so even after her untimely death at the age of 37.

In preparing this volume, the depth in which Heather Braginton-Smith touched her community, not only artistically but personally has become ever and ever more evident. This is an artist whose life as well as her paintings were her art. Slaymaker says what so many of us feel: "Heather was laughter, and she was beauty, she was love."

I am the wind that

strokes your cheek

the rain that cools your eyes

the sea that kisses your toes

pink. The tree that brings

you shade, as you too

someday will be.

Remember me.

Heather Braginton-Smith

Karen Aude, July 1997

TROMPE L'OEIL

"The hardest thing to master is the brushstroke . . . how to make those little hairs on a stick do exactly what I want them to do. It will take a life time."

Heather Braginton-Smith

Brewster Kitchen
Oil on board; 20" x 30"
Dated 1985
Private collection

The artist often took advantage of her own environment as subject, stealing
time to paint the things around her; Brewster Kitchen was her own. This
painting hung for a while in Jack's Outback in Yarmouth Port; its present
owner is unknown.

Violin with Bougereau
Oil on board; 17.5" x 37.5"
Signed and dated 1991
Private collection

*The highly polished violin hangs on a heavily grained wooden
panel on which are "pinned" family "snapshots." The caption on
one card reads "Even when I get it started, I'm not coming home."
A torn sheet of music in the bottom left hand corner begs the
viewer to smooth its wrinkled edges.*

Island Summer 1921. "Now do you believe in evolution?"
Oil on board; 6" x 8.5"
Signed and dated 1992
Collection of the Braginton-Smith family

Untitled - Peeled Lemon and Tankard
Collection unknown

*The artist's skill with paint is evident in the patinaed
surface of the beautifully rendered pewter jug.*

Untitled - Voyages and Travels
Oil on canvas; 28" x 18.5"
Dated 1995
Collection of the Braginton-Smith family

Violin, Sparrow & Rembrandt
Oil on canvas; 25" x 38"
Signed twice (upper right & lower left); dated 1989
Collection of Jill Slaymaker

Inscribed on the reverse top stretcher in the artist's hand:
"Painted in dim light. Intended to be displayed away from bright light. HEBS"

Rembrandt with Geranium
Oil on board; 12" x 16"
Signed and dated 1993
Private collection

*As a response to the artist's question to this collector to name his favorite painting,
the artist painted* Rembrandt With Geranium *in the manner of Peale.*

Mariner's Memorabilia
Collection unknown

*The meticulously painted lace and two scrimshawed whales teeth
with sailor's journal are evidence of the artist's skill with the genre.*

Masters in Art
Collection unknown

*The patinaed pewter candle holder tucked on the shelf between the seven tattered
and worn volumes is typical of the artist's series of bookshelf paintings.*

Russian Banknote
Oil on canvas; 12" x 16"
Signed and dated 1989
Private collection

The Illustrated London News
Oil on medium density overlay; 19.5" x 11.5"
Signed and dated 1993
Private collection

Free Take One
Oil on board; 10" x 15"
Signed and dated 1992
Collection of D. Teren

Jewelry Cabinet
Recycled wood; 5' 10" high x 38" wide x 20" deep
c. 1994
Private collection

A portrait of the owner painted in Elizabethan garb was rendered by the artist on a custom armoire designed and built by Cape artist Stephen Whittlesey. As the story goes, the artist had completed the commission when, on a whim, she added the small strawberry. The owner was delighted. Apparently she kept pet turtles and, unbeknownst to the artist, fed them strawberries which she had flown in to her home especially for the purpose!

LAND/SEASCAPE

"What inspires me in my art work really is my search for the truth — truth being different from honesty, which is each individual's perception of truth."

Heather Braginton-Smith

Basket of Peaches
Oil on masonite; 22" x 18"
Signed and dated 1989
Private collection

Pilot Boat *Hesper*
Oil on panel; 20" x 16"
Signed and dated 1993
Collection of Captain and Mrs Irving Gardner

The artist's friend, Jean Gardner, commissioned Pilot Boat **Hesper** *as a Christmas gift for her husband Irving, a retired Boston Harbor pilot.*

Mermaid's Keep
Oil on plywood; 23.5" x 17.5"
Signed and dated 1995
Private collection

Barnstable Harbor
Oil on birch plywood; 10" x 7"
Signed and dated 1990
Collection of the Braginton-Smith family

Dune Children
Oil on canvas; 18" x 16"
Signed and dated 1989
Collection of the Braginton-Smith family

A personal favorite of the artist, this painting hung on her kitchen wall. It features her three daughters.
The white paint spots are believed to have been accidentally splashed on the canvas by the artist.

Untitled - The Blue Wheelbarrow
Oil on board; 7.75" x 9.5"
Signed and dated 1992
Collection of Braginton-Smith family

Painted on the grounds of The Charlotte Inn on Martha's Vineyard; owner Gerret Conover was a longtime patron of the artist.

Untitled - Cat Boat
Oil on board; 10.25" x 7.25"
Signed and dated: H E Braginton-Smith © 94
Collection of Jack Braginton-Smith

The Horse Paddock
Oil on board ; 12.5' x 10.5"
Signed and dated: H E Braginton-Smith © 91
Collection of Charlotte Benner

On the back of the painting, written in the artist's hand, are the words:
"Wet Art Auction Sept 1991 – The horse paddock"

The Blockade Runner
Oil on birch panel; 9.5" x 5.5"
Signed and dated 1992
Collection of Jack Braginton-Smith

The Blockade Runner *was submitted by the artist as donation to Cape Museum of Fine Arts "Wet-Art Auction," 1992.*

HISTORIC

"The only way to develop technical mastery is to paint every day . . . to work to make the paint just squishy enough or just liquid-y enough for it to set just right. It sounds corny, but it's almost like having a romance with the paint."

Heather Braginton-Smith

Bangs Hallet
Oil on canvas; 24" x 29.5"
Dated 1989
Collection of Historical Society of Old Yarmouth

One of three historical paintings commissioned by Historical Society of Old Yarmouth to replace the originals that were stolen. The copies are widely recognized for their historic accuracy.

Amelia Hallet
Oil on canvas; 8" x 10.5"
Dated 1989
Collection of Historical Society of Old Yarmouth

*This portrait of Bangs Hallet's daughter is the second in the historic reproductions
painted by the artist when the original was stolen from the Bangs Hallet House in
Yarmouth Port.*

Asa Eldridge
Oil on canvas; 24.5" x 29.5"
Dated 1989
Collection of Historical Society of Old Yarmouth

The third in the artist's reproductions of stolen paintings from the Bangs Hallet House
in Yarmouth Port, this is a portrait of Captain Eldridge who also lived in this house.

WHIMSEY

"It is important to me that through my art I am able to take the dreams that have given me comfort and share them with other people in the hopes that they share in that same place, that same peace, that I found."

Heather Braginton-Smith

Sailors & Mermaids
Oil on canvas; 18" x 14"
Signed 'HEBS' on right-hand outside wrap; dated 1984
Collection of the Braginton-Smith family

Chocolate House with Mermaids
Oil on canvas; 18" x 14"
Dated 1984
Collection of Jack Braginton-Smith

Pen/Ink/Crayon

"I have a great kinship with a thought by Andrew Wyeth which I read recently: 'Your art goes as deep as your love goes.'"

Heather Braginton-Smith

Arien Aredhel Undomiel
#2 Pencil & 'white-out' on 60 lb rag; 7.5" x 9.5"
Unsigned and undated (Feb 1995)
Collection of ND Wiseman

Child Tying Shoes
Ink on paper; approximately 9" x 9"
Signed 1989
Collection of the Braginton-Smith family

*The artist's daughter Phillippa was model for this little black
and white drawing.*

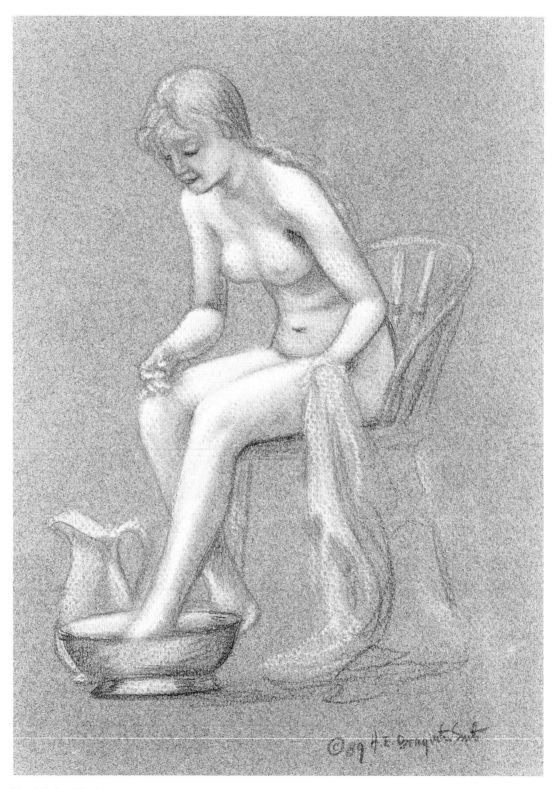

Untitled - Nude
Charcoal on paper; 7.75" x 10.5"
Signed and dated 1989

Untitled - Nude
Charcoal and pastel pencil on paper; 8" x 11.75"
Signed and dated 1989

All the above black and white pencil sketches are commercial drawings rendered by the artist for Puritan of Cape Cod.

STILL LIFE

"People can focus on the negative in art, which has great power. but so does the depth of realism and richness or softness of color that I can use to represent the presence of love, which is what lasts — and the peace that comes with it."

Heather Braginton-Smith

Still-Life with Gourd & Grapes
Oil on plywood; 13" x 11"
Signed and dated 1995
Collection of Jack Braginton-Smith

Strawberries
Oil on board; 8.5" x 5.75"
Signed and dated: H E Braginton-Smith © 92
Private collection.

Homage to the Old Apple Tree
Oil on canvas; 16" x 12"
Signed and dated 1988
Collection of Mimi and Warren McConchie

Remarks on the back in Heather's hand read:
The last harvested fruit from Deacon Joseph's old apple tree, "and one golden plum." My great old shady friend, children gathered
your fruit and played in your shade, and I've remembered you. (signed) "H. 88 Nobscussett"

Brewster collector Warren McConchie remembers his first meeting with the artist: "It was at the 1988 Cape Museum of Fine Arts
'Wet Art Auction' that I first met Heather. A young lady approached me and said, 'You bought my Deacon Joseph's Apple Tree.' We
introduced ourselves and I told her how pleased I was to be the high bidder because I admired this painting so much. 'Well, Warren,'
she said, 'You made a very wise choice, because one day I am going to be famous.' "In that case, I said, I will keep it forever. Heather
and I went on to become good Friends."

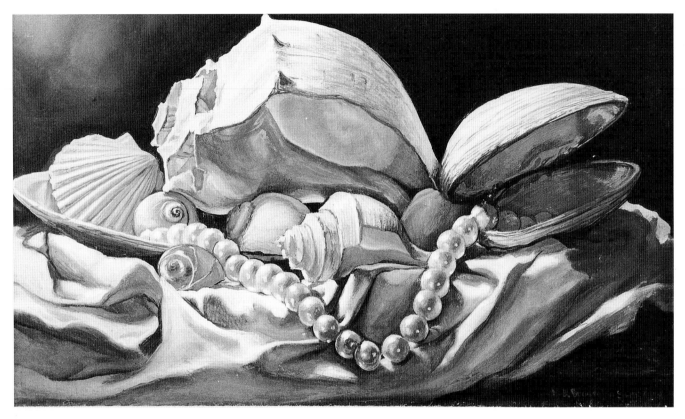

Untitled — Shells with Pearl Necklace on Satin
Oil on board; 9.5" x 5.5"
Signed and dated 1993
Collection of the Braginton-Smith family

Still-Life with Yellow Gourd & Sunflower
Oil on plywood; 9" x 12"
Unsigned and undated (c. 1995)
Collection of Jack Braginton-Smith

Still Life with Peaches and Blueberry Muffin
Oil on board; 14.5" x 14.5"
Dated 1989
Collection of the Braginton-Smith family

Edgeworth Plug Slice
Oil on plywood; 7" x 7"
Signed and dated 1990
Collection of Mimi and Warren McConchie

SHOWHOUSE

Show House is an annual fundraiser put on by The Junior League of Boston. It is a major area happening. Heather Braginton-Smith was invited to participate in the 1997 Show House and was in the process of completing her hallway mural just prior to her death. In tribute to her, The Junior League of Boston dedicated its 1997 Show House to the artist.

"Heather inspired us with her talent, dedication, and wonderful sense of humor. Upon entering the Show House all are greeted by her beautiful mural that fills the house with a sense of warmth and serenity.

Heather shared her gifts with the members of the Junior League of Boston for a short time and touched all those who have been a part of the 1997 Show House.

We will remember her fondly."

The artist's decorative painting combined many of her talents from trompe l'oeil to still life and scenic design.

As was usual with the artist, she often used her own children as models in her work. Here, the dark-haired cherub on the left resembles the artist's son Joshua.

Details of the Show House mural reveal elements of the artist's humor. Here a cherub tumbles, feet dangling off the faux molding.

PORTRAIT

"I am inspired by the idea that through my art I can love people and give them that feeling of peace that comes with love. Not romantic love which so often brings us pain, but rather that love we knew as children that kept our trust safe and quiet and alive."

Heather Braginton-Smith

Child with Cat
Oil on canvas; 16" x 16"
Signed and dated 1989
Collection of the Braginton-Smith family

Erendis Of Númenorë
Oil on medium density overlay; 14" x 17"
Signed and dated (October)1993
Dedication and personal inscription on reverse.
Collection of ND Wiseman

Tentatively titled "The Letter," it wasn't until June of 1994 that the artist asked a friend to tell her its story, she having painted the painting on a whim. The friend regaled the artist with the tale of Erendis of Emerië, Lady of the Star Island of Númenorë, and her patient love for the ever-absent mariner Prince Aldarion of Armenelos. A long and bittersweet story of love and redemption, the coveted letter from Aldarion that Erendis holds is filled with much news of far-distant shores, but little concerning his eventual return. She sits gazing out to sea, waiting, perhaps in vain, to catch the first glimpse of his legendary ship.

Woman with Necklace
Oil on canvas; 14 x 18
Signed, but not dated (1989)
Collection of the Braginton-Smith family

This is a copy of an original work painted on panel and dated 1775. The sheet on the reverse reads in part: "A fine example of trompe l'oeil. This and the original are identical in clarity, save on close inspection. The original bears museum marks on the back, and this is the only known copy."

Portrait of a Young Man
Oil on canvas; 10" x 14"
Signed, but not dated (c. 1974)
Collection of the Braginton-Smith family

Remarks on the reverse top stretcher, written in the artist's hand, read:
"Portrait of a young man by Bronzino. Oil on canvas (signed) Heather Braginton-Smith.
Painted in 'The Pit.' Mrs Hopkins." (Mrs Pauline Hopkins was the art teacher at
Dennis-Yarmouth Regional High School for many years and one of the people the artist
credited with encouraging her interest in art.)

58 **Self-Portrait: Aged Seventeen**
Oil on canvas; 22" x 28"
Unsigned and undated (1976)
Collection of Jack Braginton-Smith

Reading Jane Eyre
Oil on medium density overlay; 15" x 11.25"
Signed and dated: H E Braginton-Smith 94
Private collection

Mademoiselle Balletti
Oil on birch panel; 18" x 23"
Unsigned and undated (c.1991)
Collection of the Braginton-Smith family

*This painting is rendered in the style of a painting
by Jean Marc Natere, 1757.*

Untitled - Alexandra
Dated 1986
Collection of Braginton-Smith family

*The artist's eldest daughter, then aged three, sits with
her cat for this family portrait.*

Inner Portraits

"Rather than painting a portrait of what a person looks like, I paint the things they love and the people they love."

Heather Braginton-Smith

For the Love of Walter
Oil on panel; 17" x 13"
Dated 1990
Collection of Mr. and Mrs. Walter Cronkite

*The artist was commissioned to paint this inner portrait of retired newscaster Walter
Cronkite who describes the painting as "absolutely marvelous and filled with some of
our favorite artifacts." Among them Cronkite affectionately mentions his pet cat. Bits of
navigational equipment and books speak to Cronkite's interests in things nautical.*

Masterpiece Theatre
17.5" x 23.5"
Dated 1991
Collection of the Vincent Price estate

This poster-sized inner portrait was used by WGBH Channel 2 Boston to commemorate the 20th anniversary of the Masterpiece Theatre television show and the 10th anniversary of Mystery, and as a tribute to Vincent Price, host of "Mystery" in those days, and of Alastaire Cooke. Mr. Price was thrilled with the painting and wrote a personal thank you to the artist. Mr. Cooke had declined to send a portrait from which his likeness might be rendered, but the artist, not to be thwarted, painted a miniature Alastaire Cooke on the skeleton key. Not content, she also painted a tiny mouse hiding in a hole, nibbling on a cookie that says something about the key. This was typical of the artist's often tongue-in-cheek humor. Her painting itself was a treasure hunt mystery, in keeping with its commissioned purpose.

Dr. Robert D. Ballard: An Inner Portrait
Oil on birch plywood; 28" x 19"
Signed and dated 1994
Collection of Dr. and Mrs. Robert D. Ballard

*Commissioned by the Ballards, this inner portrait features little portraits of Dr. and Mrs.
Ballard's children. Included also are bits and pieces of importance to the couple such as the
rendering of the Tiki or Polyneasian god and a portait of the Nautilus, one of Dr. Ballard's
favorite vessels.*

Fantasy and Myth

"Difficult experiences in my past personal life have manifested my love in different ways through my artwork. My fantasy art pieces were my place to be, where I kept my love and my belief in the beautiful alive. I was able to wander in that world and take my dreams and make them visually real — and keep them alive that way."

Heather Braginton-Smith

Pops-By-The-Sea
Oil on wood panel; 17" x 23"
Signed and dated 1989
Private collection
(Photograph is of limited edition lithograph.)

*In 1989 the artist was chosen by the Arts
Foundation of Cape Cod (AFCC) to render
a painting in celebration of its annual concert.
The original was auctioned to benefit AFCC;
a limited edition of prints was also published.*

*The accompanying poem reads:
It happened not so long ago, perhaps not
so far away, when one man's music
became so pure and clear, it called forth
enchantment of ages past, bewitched by
the beauty of the song, unseen, but
present always in the heart.*

The Gift of the Rose
Oil on board; 8.75" x 11.5"
Signed and dated 1990
Collection of Katherine Kingman Wooster

*This painting is said to have been one of the artist's
favorites. It depicts a beautiful woman clutching a rose to
herself, a gift from her lover whose boat can be seen sailing
off in the distance. The parting, according to the artist's story
of her painting, caused her to change back into a mermaid.*

The Conversation
Oil on wood panel; 17.5" x 23.5"
Signed and dated 1993
Private collection

Merchild
Oil on birch panel; 8.5" x 7"
Signed and dated 1989
Private collection

This painting is a forerunner of the the artist's later and more illustrative "Mermaid" series. The artist often used her children as models; daughter Johanna is depicted here as the Merchild. The owner of the painting believes it was in many ways also a self portrait: "Merchild always reminds me of Heather with her arms wrapped back looking to the stars—to me, that expressed Heather."

The Fisherman's Wife
Oil on panel; 8.5" x 11"
Signed and dated 1989
Collection of Jack Braginton-Smith

*The partial story written on the reverse of the
painting in the artist's hand reads as follows:*

*The old fisherman brought her back to
his wife—this orphaned child of the sea.*

*With painstaking care the old woman crafted
a baby's dress of her fine linen. Her favorite
old paisley scarf was sacrificed to trim the little
mermaid of the rocks.*

*So angelic was the child, the old woman's heart
was filled again with the love of all lost
memory. And with stern and loving kindness,
she raised her to her own.*

*(The artist's oldest daughter, Alexandra, then
aged seven was the model for the Merchild.)*

The Mercy
Oil on birch panel; 12" x 10"
Signed and dated 1987
Private collection

69

*This is the original, little-known version of the artist's painting
titled* The Gift of the Great Pearl *painted in 1988*

The Captive
Oil on Masonite; 18" x 24"
Signed and dated 1987
Collection of Brian and Nancy Braginton-Smith

The Grotto
Oil on masonite; 20" x 24"
Signed and undated (1987)
Collection of Brian and Nancy Braginton-Smith

*The best compositionally of the three fantasy illustrations
offered here, this piece, while true to the genre, shows both
a departure and a budding mastery of the formulas of her
predecessors.*

Ametra's Quest
Acrylite and oil on canvas panel; 16" x 20"
Signed and dated 1991
Private collection

The Lookout
Oil on wood panel; 8" x 6"
Signed and dated 1988
Collection of Mimi and Warren McConchie

The Witch of Billingsgate
Oil & acrylic on canvas; 41.5" x 27.5"
Signed and dated 1989
Private collection

The artist was inspired to paint Witches of Billingsgate *after listening to Enya's first album. One piece, which she played over and over again, symbolized longing to the artist who translated this feeling into her painting represented by the witch's longing as the ship went down.*

SCULPTURE

"Look to the sea, old man .... Here, in the sea....

He squinted in a gaze intended, not for the surface waters, but down,

down to the depths. He saw two children of the sea. Their sleek tails of

rich, dark blues and greens, blending into the opalescence of their skins."

excerpt from a story by Heather Braginton-Smith

Mermaid
Clay figure on marble base
10.25" high (mermaid 8" from tail to head)
Painted black and green faux marble to match base
Dated 1995
Collection of David Callander

CHECKLIST

The whereabouts of several of the paintings reproduced in this catalogue are unknown.
Anyone with additional information on any of these or other paintings by Heather
Braginton-Smith is invited to contact the publisher at the address on the last page
of this catalog to help assist in a more complete cataloging of the artist's work.

Page # **TROMPE L'OEIL**

10 Brewster Kitchen
Oil on board; 20" x 30"
Dated 1985
Private collection

11 Violin with Bougereau
Oil on board; 17.5" x 37.5"
Signed and dated 1991
Private collection

12 Island Summer 1921
Oil on board; 6" x 8.5"
Signed and dated 1992
Collection of the Braginton-Smith family

13 Untitled - Peeled Lemon and Tankard
Collection unknown

13 Untitled - Voyages and Travels
Oil on canvas; 28" x 18.5"
Dated 1995
Collection of the Braginton-Smith family

14 Violin, Sparrow & Rembrandt
Oil on canvas; 25" x 38"
Signed twice (upper right & lower left); dated 1989
Collection of Jill Slaymaker

15 Rembrandt with Geranium
Oil on board; 12" x 16"
Dated 1993
Private collection

16 Mariner's Memorabilia
Collection unknown

16 Masters in Art
Collection unknown

17 Russian Banknote
Oil on canvas; 12" x 16"
Signed and dated 1989
Private collection

18 The Illustrated London News
Oil on medium density overlay; 19.5" x 11.5"
Signed and dated 1993
Private collection

19 Free Take One
Oil on board; 10" x 15"
Signed and dated 1992
Collection of D. Teren

20 Jewelry Cabinet
Recycled wood; 5' 10" high x 38" wide x 20" deep
c. 1994
Private collection

LAND/SEASCAPE

22 Basket of Peaches
Oil on masonite; 22" x 18"
Signed and dated 1989
Private collection

23 Pilot Boat *Hesper*
Oil on panel; 20" x 16"
Signed and dated 1993
Collection of Captain and Mrs. Irving Gardner

24 Mermaid's Keep
Oil on plywood; 23.5" x 17.5"
Signed and dated 1995
Private collection

24 Barnstable Harbor
Oil on birch plywood; 10" x 7"
Signed and dated 1990
Collection of the Braginton-Smith family

25 Dune Children
Oil on canvas; 18" x 16"
Signed and dated 1989
Collection of the Braginton-Smith family

26 Untitled - The Blue Wheelbarrow
Oil on board; 7.75" x 9.5"
Signed and dated 1992
Collection of Braginton-Smith family

27 Untitled - Cat Boat
Oil on board; 10.25" x 7.25"
Signed and dated: H E Braginton-Smith © 94
Collection of Jack Braginton-Smith

27 The Horse Paddock
Oil on board ; 12.5' x 10.5"
Signed and dated: H E Braginton-Smith © 91
Collection of Charlotte Benner.

28   **The Blockade Runner**
      Oil on birch panel; 9.5" x 5.5"
      Signed and dated 1992
      Collection of Jack Braginton-Smith

      ## HISTORICAL

30   **Bangs Hallet**
      Oil on canvas; 24" x 29.5"
      Dated 1989
      Collection of Historical Society of Old Yarmouth

31   **Amelia Hallet**
      Oil on canvas; 8" x 10.5"
      Dated 1989
      Collection of Historical Society of Old Yarmouth

32   **Asa Eldridge**
      Oil on canvas; 24.5" x 29.5"
      Dated 1989
      Collection of Historical Society of Old Yarmouth

      ## WHIMSEY

34   **Sailors & Mermaids**
      Oil on canvas; 18" x 14"
      Signed 'HEBS' on right-hand outside wrap; dated 1984
      Collection of the Braginton-Smith family

34   **Chocolate House with Mermaids**
      Oil on canvas; 18" x 14"
      Dated 1984
      Collection of Jack Braginton-Smith

      ## PEN/INK/CRAYON

36   **Arien Aredhel Undomiel**
      #2 Pencil & 'white-out' on 60 lb rag; 7.5" x 9.5"
      Unsigned and undated (Feb 1995)
      Collection of ND Wiseman

37   **Child Tying Shoes**
      Ink on paper; approximately 9" x 9"
      Signed 1989
      Collection of the Braginton-Smith family

38   **Untitled - Nude**
      Charcoal on paper; 7.75" x 10.5"
      Signed and dated 1989

39   **Untitled - Nude**
      Charcoal and pastel pencil on paper; 8" x 11.75"
      Signed and dated 1989

40   **Pencil sketches for Puritan of Cape Cod**
      Collection of Puritan of Cape Cod

      ## STILL LIFE

42   **Still-Life with Gourd & Grapes**
      Oil on plywood; 13" x 11"
      Signed and dated 1995
      Collection of Jack Braginton-Smith

43   **Strawberries**
      Oil on board; 8.5" x 5.75"
      Signed and dated: H E Braginton-Smith © 92
      Private collection

44   **Homage to the Old Apple Tree**
      Oil on canvas; 16" x 12"
      Signed and dated 1988
      Collection of Mimi and Warren McConchie

45   **Untitled — Shells with Pearl Necklace on Satin**
      Oil on board; 9.5" x 5.5"
      Signed and dated 1993
      Collection of the Braginton-Smith family

46   **Still-Life with Yellow Gourd & Sunflower**
      Oil on plywood; 9" x 12"
      Unsigned and undated (c. 1995)
      Collection of Jack Braginton-Smith

47   **Still Life with Peaches and Blueberry Muffin**
      Oil on board; 14.5" x 14.5"
      Dated 1989
      Collection of the Braginton-Smith family

48   **Edgeworth Plug Slice**
      Oil on plywood; 7" x 7"
      Signed and dated 1990
      Collection of Mimi and Warren McConchie

49-52 ## SHOWHOUSE

      ## PORTRAIT

54   **Child with Cat**
      Oil on canvas; 16" x 16"
      Signed and dated 1989
      Collection of the Braginton-Smith family

55   **Erendis Of Númenorë**
      Oil on medium density overlay; 14" x 17"
      Signed and dated (October)1993
      Dedication and personal inscription on reverse.
      Collection of ND Wiseman

56   **Woman with Necklace**
      Oil on canvas; 14 x 18
      Signed, but not dated (1989)
      Collection of the Braginton-Smith family

57   **Portrait of a Young Man**
      Oil on canvas; 10" x 14"
      Signed, but not dated (c. 1974)
      Collection of the Braginton-Smith family

58   **Self-Portrait: Aged Seventeen**
      Oil on canvas; 22" x 28"
      Unsigned and undated (1976)
      Collection of Jack Braginton-Smith

59   **Reading Jane Eyre**
      Oil on medium density overlay; 15" x 11.25"
      Signed and dated: H E Braginton-Smith 94
      Private collection

60   **Mademoiselle Balletti**
      Oil on birch panel; 18" x 23"
      Unsigned and undated (c.1991)
      Collection of the Braginton-Smith family

60   **Untitled - Alexandra**
      Dated 1986
      Collection of Braginton-Smith family

INNER PORTRAIT

62   **For the Love of Walter**
      Oil on panel; 17" x 13"
      Dated 1990
      Collection of Mr. and Mrs. Walter Cronkite

63   **Masterpiece Theatre**
      17.5" x 23.5"
      Dated 1991
      Collection of the Vincent Price estate

64   **Dr. Robert D. Ballard: An Inner Portrait**
      Oil on birch plywood; 28" x 19"
      Signed and dated 1994
      Collection of Dr. and Mrs. Robert D. Ballard

FANTASY AND MYTH

66   **Pops-By-The-Sea**
      Oil on wood panel; 17" x 23"
      Signed and dated 1989
      Private collection

66   **The Gift of the Rose**
      Oil on board; 8.75" x 11.5"
      Signed and dated 1990
      Collection of Katherine Kingman Wooster

67   **The Conversation**
      Oil on wood panel; 17.5" x 23.5"
      Signed and dated 1993
      Private collection

68   **Merchild**
      Oil on birch panel; 8.5" x 7"
      Signed and dated 1989
      Private collection

69   **The Fisherman's Wife**
      Oil on panel; 8.5" x 11"
      Signed and dated 1989
      Collection of Jack Braginton-Smith

69   **The Mercy**
      Oil on birch panel; 12" x 10"
      Signed and dated 1987
      Private collection

70   **The Captive**
      Oil on Masonite; 18" x 24"
      Signed and dated 1987
      Collection of Brian and Nancy Braginton-Smith

70   **The Grotto**
      Oil on masonite; 20" x 24"
      Signed and undated (1987)
      Collection of Brian and Nancy Braginton-Smith

71   **Ametra's Quest**
      Acrylite and oil on canvas panel; 16" x 20"
      Signed and dated 1991
      Private collection

72   **The Lookout**
      Oil on wood panel; 8" x 6"
      Signed and dated 1988
      Collection of Mimi and Warren McConchie

72   **The Witch of Billingsgate**
      Oil & acrylic on canvas; 41.5" x 27.5"
      Signed and dated 1989
      Private collection

SCULPTURE

74   **Mermaid**
      Clay figure on marble base
      10.25" high (mermaid 8" from tail to head)
      Painted black and green faux marble to match base
      Dated 1995
      Collection of David Callandar

© 1997 by DECAL PUBLISHING
P.O. Box 65
Yarmouth Port, MA 02675

Edited by Karen Aude
Design by Weatherbee Design

Photography by

Gary Andrashko
(pages: 12, 13, 18, 20, 25, 26, 27, 30, 31, 32, 38, 39,
40, 43, 45, 47, 54, 59, 60, 63, 66, 70, 72, 74)

ND Wiseman
(pages: 14, 23, 24, 25, 28, 34, 36, 37, 42,
44, 46, 48, 55, 56, 57, 58, 68, 69, 71,)

Christopher Green (page 67)

Printing by O'Brien & Company Printers, Inc.
Special thanks to the Cape Museum of Fine Arts for their assistance.